The Essence of SIKHISM

The Lives and Teachings of the Sikh Gurus

(Mrs) T. K. Anand, M.A. B.Ed.
*Formerly Principal, Guru Nanak Public School
Punjabi Bagh/Pitampura, New Delhi
Formerly Senior Supervisor, Guru Harkrishan Public School
India Gate, New Delhi*

VIKAS PUBLISHING HOUSE PVT LTD
576 Masjid Road, Jangpura, New Delhi 110 014 Ph. 4314605, 4315313
Email: chawlap@giasdl01.vsnl.net.in Fax: 91-11-327 6593
http://www.ubspd.com

First Floor, N.S. Bhawan, 4th Cross, 4th Main,
Gandhi Nagar, Bangalore 560009 Ph. 2204639

Distributors:
UBS PUBLISHERS' DISTRIBUTORS LTD
- 5, Ansari Road, **New Delhi**-110002 Ph. 3273601, 3266646
- Apeejay Chambers, 5 Wallace St., **Mumbai**-400001 Ph. 2070827, 2076971
- 10, First Main Road, Gandhi Nagar, **Bangalore**-560009 Ph. 2263901
- 6, Sivaganga Road, Nungambakkam, **Chennai**-600034 Ph. 8276355
- 8/1-B, Chowringhee Lane, **Calcutta**-700016 Ph. 2441821, 2442910
- 5-A, Rajendra Nagar, **Patna**- 800016 Ph. 652856, 656169
- 80, Noronha Road, Cantonment, **Kanpur**-208004 Ph. 369124, 362665

Copyright © Vikas Publishing House Pvt Ltd, 1996

Reprint, 1998

Illustrated by : S.P. Singh

All rights reserved. No part of this publication may be reproduced in any form without the prior written permission of the publishers.

Laser Typeset by Alfa Computer Centre, Delhi.
Printed at   TARA ART PRINTERS, , Noida, U.P.

Preface

As the communication revolution reduces the world to a 'Global Village,' the most compelling issue before educationists is to enable students to discover a moral axis within themselves. This axis is vital for balancing the rapidity of change in modern times with the stability of an omnipotent soul force. The lives and teachings of the Sikh Gurus are a remarkable exposition of the moral axis within ourselves. These teachings are an excellent medium whereby students can face the multifaceted challenges of the modern world with sublime courage and a sense of direction towards a clear goal.

Having taught for three decades, and led a Sikh public school as a principal for more than fifteen years, I have made this compendium an evolutionary process, clearly keeping in view the gradual development of a child's age, and keeping an eye on the time allotted for Divinity classes. Useful exercises have been provided at the end of every chapter in each book in order to help the students to recapitulate the historical setting of a story told, or to understand the deeper truth enshrined in the teachings of the ten Masters.

In my teaching career, I have taught right from tiny tots through higher classes, to senior secondary level where young boys and girls enter the threshold of adult life. This series is a humble offering by me before the eternally living Guru, Guru Granth Sahib, from out of the experience of an entire life devoted to education.

(Mrs) T.K. Anand

ਮੂਲ ਮੰਤਰ
(Mool Mantra)

ੴ
Ek Onkar
God Is One.

ਸਤਿਨਾਮੁ ਕਰਤਾ ਪੁਰਖੁ
Sat(i) Nām(u) kartā Purakh

ਨਿਰਭਉ ਨਿਰਵੈਰੁ
Nirbhau nirvair(u)
He is without fear,
He is without enemity.

ਅਕਾਲ ਮੂਰਤਿ ਅਜੂਨੀ
Akal murāt(i) Ajuni
He is timeless,
He is beyond births and deaths

ਸੈਭੰ ਗੁਰ ਪ੍ਰਸਾਦਿ ॥
Saibhang Gur Prasād(i)
He is self illuminated,
He is realized by the kindness of the true Guru.

॥ ਜਪੁ ॥
Jap(u)
Repeat His Name.

ਆਦਿ ਸਚੁ ਜੁਗਾਦਿ ਸਚੁ ॥
Ad(i) Sach(u) jugad(u) Sach
He was true before the beginning,
He was true when the ages began.

ਹੈ ਭੀ ਸਚੁ
Hai bhi sach(u)

ਨਾਨਕ ਹੋਸੀ ਭੀ ਸਚੁ ॥੧॥
Nanak hosi bhi sach(u)
He existeth now, says Nanak,
and shall exist forever.

Contents

1. Our First Guru 7
2. Our Second Guru 8
3. Our Third Guru 9
4. Our Fourth Guru 10
5. Our Fifth Guru 11
6. Our Sixth Guru 12
7. Our Seventh Guru 13
8. Our Eighth Guru 14
9. Our Ninth Guru 15
10. Our Tenth Guru 16
11. Our Present Guru 17
12. Gurdwara 18
13. The Golden Temple 20
14. Ek Onkar 22
15. Khanda 23
16. Five K's (Kakkas) 24
17. The Khalsa Flag 26
    How Much Do You Remember ?. 27

1. Our First Guru

Guru Nanak Dev Ji

His father's name was Mehta Kalu.
His mother's name was Mata Tripta.
He was born at Talwandi.

2. Our Second Guru

Guru Angad Dev Ji

His father's name was Pherumal. His mother's name was Daya Kaur. He was born at Harika, a village in Ferozepur District.

3. Our Third Guru

Guru Amardas Ji

His father's name was Tej Bhan.
His mother's name was Bakht Kaur.
He was born at Basarka,
a village in Amritsar District.

4. Our Fourth Guru

Guru Ram Das Ji

His father's name was Hari Das.
His mother's name was Daya Kaur.
He was born at Lahore.

5. Our Fifth Guru

Guru Arjan Dev Ji

His father was Guru Ram Das ji. His mother's name was Mata Bhani. He was born at Goindwal.

6. Our Sixth Guru

Guru Hargobind Ji

His father was Guru Arjan Dev ji.
His mother's name was Mata Ganga.
He was born at Wadali,
a village in Amritsar District.

7. Our Seventh Guru

Guru Har Rai Ji

His father's name was Baba Gurditta.
His mother's name was Nihal Kaur.
He was born at Kiratpur.

8. Our Eighth Guru

Guru Harkrishan Ji

His father was Guru Har Rai ji.
His mother's name was Kishan Kaur.
He was born at Kiratpur.

9. Our Ninth Guru

Guru Tegh Bahadur Ji

His father was Guru Hargobind ji.
His mother's name was Nanki.
He was born at Amritsar.

10. Our Tenth Guru

Guru Gobind Singh Ji

His father was Guru Tegh Bahadur ji. His mother's name was Mata Gujri. He was born at Patna.

11. Our Present Guru

Guru Granth Sahib Ji

Guru Granth Sahib ji was compiled by the fifth Guru — Guru Arjan Dev ji to guide the Sikhs.

12. Gurdwara

Gurdwara Bangla Sahib

a) Sikhs pray in a Gurdwara.
b) Hindus pray in a Temple.
c) Muslims pray in a Mosque.
d) Christians pray in a Church.
e) Gurdwara means Guru's home.
f) Guru Granth Sahib is kept in all the Gurdwaras.
g) Some Sikhs have Gurdwaras at home (known as Babaji's room).

13. The Golden Temple

a) The Golden Temple is a place of pilgrimage for the Sikhs.
b) It is in Amritsar.
c) It is also called Harmandar Sahib or Darbar Sahib.

14. Ek Onkar

a) It is an important symbol.
b) Guru Granth Sahib starts with Ek Onkar.
c) It means — God Is One.

15. Khanda

a) Khanda is the emblem of the Khalsa.
b) It has a two edged sword in the middle.
c) It has an iron ring around the two edged sword.
d) It has a sword on each side of the ring.

16. Five K's (Kakkas)

These are the five symbols given to the Sikhs by the tenth Guru - Guru Gobind Singh ji.
a) Kesh: uncut hair
b) Kangha: comb
c) Kachcha: short drawer
d) Kara: iron bangle
e) Kirpan: small sword

17. The Khalsa Flag

Nishan Sahib

a) Its colour is orange (saffron).
b) It is triangular in shape.
c) It has a Khanda drawn in black.
d) The flag post is covered with orange (saffron) coloured cloth.
e) One can see Nishan Sahib from far.
f) All the Gurdwaras have Nishan Sahib.

How Much Do You Remember ?

1. Write the names of the ten Gurus. Collect and paste their pictures:

2. Collect pictures of the ten Gurus and paste them in the correct order.

3. Complete Nishan Sahib and colour it.

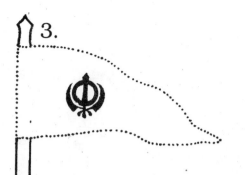

4. Fill in the blanks :
   a) Sikhs pray in a _____.
   b) Hindus pray in a _____.
   c) Muslims pray in a _____.
   d) Christians pray in a _____.
   e) Golden Temple is in _____.
   f) The Khalsa flag is called _____.
   g) The colour of the Khalsa flag is _____.
   h) The Khalsa emblem is called _____.

5. Name the five K's (kakkas) and complete and label the following pictures :

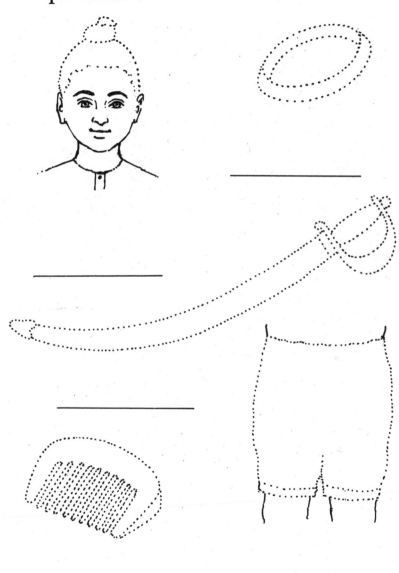

6. Collect the pictures of the important Gurdwaras in Delhi and paste them below :